The Fourth Part of

Love

By

Markeith A. Wilson Jr.

ISBN: 978-1-951300-74-6

Liberation's Publishing LLC ~ West Point, Mississippi

Table of Contents

Dedication

For SHANÈE

Giving You My Fourths

Held down my best round, hopefully

I don't have to fight with you.

Giving the circumstances I can understand it if

you have a lil doubt or two.

Giving my past and my present

I'm able to dang near dance at the sight of you.

Give you my heart by the fourths cause it's under reconstruction

and I see by the way you blushin that you wanna give more than a half or two.

Honestly, I'm feeling you.

Mentally I'm hip to you showing it by holding my hand out just to give to you.

Glad it wound up the way it did.

Hopefully, this leads to us having sense enough to know if it's wrong or right.

Hope it don't keep us awake at night

cause we gone need all our energy to be complete.

I don't need you getting tired with me.

so, I hold out on a few surprises and moments.

Hoping it leads to our best times and favorite moments

giving enough time we'll be head over hills.

Not letting the day pass without one of us calling to head over

for hugs and kisses deeper wishes turn to fantasies that come true

you dreamed half your life that you'd be with someone you love

and now those dreams come true

After All

I don't want you to leave me stranded in my thoughts.

I just wish that you would be standing after all my faults.

Cause I don't want to be alone at night,

Looking at the sky all by myself.

I don't mind it if we fuss and fight,

As long as you're here at the end of the night.

I'm at the point where I can't bear to lose you.

Don't pay too much mind to everything I do.

I was damaged.

I wasn't over my past and I couldn't stand it.

It just happened to be your lips that made me feel.

It just happened to be your love that feels so real.

And I don't know how to deal.

Let's just be honest.

I'm a guy that just keeps on running into the same old hurt.

But that won't keep me from you.

You got a heart worth fighting for and

I'm gone try it just let me warn you.

I want you to still be standing after all my faults.

I don't need you to leave me hanging after all I saw.

Let's keep on dreaming.

You just keep on being too good to be true,

Stay breathing.

Because I want you to be here, so I'll never be gone.

Let me hold you when you can't be strong.

I'm damaged, but I'm still a rock to lean on.

Even though I'm damaged I can still be your soulmate.

If you're damaged, I don't mind putting together pieces long as I can.

I just want to be sure that we'll still be standing after all our faults.

Before I Knew It

Kissed an Angel before I knew it.

Held her heart before I knew it.

Fell in love before I knew it.

She let her thoughts unfold and right there I knew it.

My dreams had come to me.

Lights inside my darkness have lit my thoughts up.

Giving me new energy and motivation for everything

How could it be what could this be?

Is it true that fantasy could become reality or am I still dreaming?

Scared to touch or get pinched in fear that I might awake.

Only to get both at the same time

But you look me in the eyes and reassure me that you're real.

And just like that

Angels are real before I knew it.

Love was real before I knew it.

Her heart grew in with mine before I knew it.

Just like that I chose to change before I knew it.

Something so divine and at its truest

Your love was a foreign tongue but now I speak it fluent.

Cause everything, I ever dreamed of came true because of you.

and it happened before I knew it.

The Silence in the Loud Place

Past thoughts...

"I knew I ought to try to love even after heartbreak."

I'd need a golden calculator to calculate the time it'd take to try again.

From the pain we felt, to the time we've spent, I pondered when.

When would I try again to give into feelings of love?

Since I've been alone, I knew that wasn't the goal.

I could conquer the world,

but what good is the world if didn't have love.

At least someone capable of loving genuinely, deeply.

More so from the soul than from the mind.

Is there such a soul, such a spirit that could take place in a woman.

There has to be.

In time I thought I'd find this queen and I'd make her my own

But where would she be, where could she hide?

the thoughts resided in my mind.

until...

one day at work of all places.

I felt her soul first,

and then I saw her face.

in such a loud place everything went quiet.

A silence that I'd never experienced.

The type of calm after a storm and at that moment I knew.

I found my queen.

Love Is

You've given me love.

In the purest form

I heard every word you said when you said,

you wouldn't break my heart.

Loving from my heart to yours a bond

that I pray never ever need any time apart

Your loving keeps me showing out.

Even when it's just you and me I want to show you off.

Cause your love is so sincere I thank God for allowing me to be with you right here
and experience how your love is

In my eyes so perfect love like this is worth all the other times I stayed up hurting.

Now I look into this love you give it's true.

Its more than a little new it's like a dream come true.

Just to sit with you and review this time we've spent loving.

From my heart to yours love and you love me of course.

I can't wait until the day where I can say I want that hand of yours

Passion

That's what she made me feel.

My heart never went astray.

If this was my last day with her, I can say she made me feel passion.

In some shape or form

Love from a caring lover is what she says she's on

I'm sure she's mine my very own

But not to own but to stand beside and carry on.

My future that's my key to home.

But all I really want to know is if I make her feel Passion.

Giving my light you glow; your smile is wow.

As beautiful as a sunset so

I hope it Don't go down don't let my day end.

This is the type of daydream that you'd want to stay in

This is a yacht you get aboard even if you can't swim.

A fear of drowning goes away because you'll be safe.

So long as you feel passion.

A feeling like no other as you continue.

to show each other who you are.

She'll unveil the reason she glows now.

The reason why she's so proud to go out.

The reason she picks you up when you're down.

To kiss your lips if you frown

The real reason she sticks around.

Is because you turned her world upside down.

A feeling she claims to not be able to live without

She said I made her feel passion.

Reasons for Rainbows

You're like my rain cloud and my sunshine at the same time.

Baby you're the reason rainbows appear.

Holding on to my first mind for the last time

I'm giving you all I got my dear

This time I'm gone be fine cause before you I faced all my fears.

Tears running in my hands thoughts just racing in my head.

I don't want to have to lay alone in bed.

So, from this day forth till I'm dead I'll give you all I can.

For as long as I can bear

Cause baby you're like my rain cloud and my sunshine.

at the same time

Baby you're the reason rainbows appear.

After all the storm and the rain, I can finally feel love again.

Finally, I can be more than just friends.

And trust my heart in yours and then,

Let the water pour on our souls to create love and happiness.

I love who I've become and the woman you've been for me.

Its crazy cause I never thought I'd meet somebody who'd be my

Rain cloud and my sunshine at the same time

I never knew you'd be the reason rainbows appeared.

Today

I thought about you today.

I felt like it should be just me and you today.

I really think I should make my best move today.

Get rich just so I can drape you up in jewels today.

I just want to tell you I love you and kiss your lips today.

Grab your body and caress you by the hips today.

I feel like I should put on a slow jam and dance the night away.

Go to a movie and walk under the sunlight while I admire you today.

I got in my feelings and felt like writing about you today.

I want to take the day off sit you down and say it's all about you today.

Spoil you and tell you it's us against the world.

As long as you'll be my girl.

I'll shine the light and take the pain away.

To the best of my abilities, I'll love you today.

And tomorrow and the next and so on so long as I have breath.

Give you love and make the best of what life we've been given.

I love you and that much is a given.

But today is different.

I wanted to let you know especially if your vision doesn't see it clearly.

I love you so I took the time out today for you.

Truth and Lies

I got a handful of your truths and lies.

I got a heart filled with your name plus mine.

I got mind full of your lips and eyes.

I can't help but see you when I close my eyes.

I just can't shake this vibe.

It's like you could be mine but I gotta be the first one to say hey.

You could be mine, but I have to be the first one to be great.

And I gotta be the best me I can be so I can be the last guy that you date.

Hopefully, I'm your type, cause if not this might be the worst shot that I take.

This is like a first crush no words when you get in my face.

It's always the wrong words when I'm trying to say hey.

But I finally got the courage just to ask you out and I hope I don't freeze.

I hope you don't leave me stranded in my thoughts.

Never knowing what loving you is all about

You interest me hopefully you're just as interested.

The way that you look at me is all to innocent.

Say yes and I'll be there on time first dates on me.

The first impression is key so hopefully.

You say yes.

What I see In Your Eyes

In your eyes I see passion

An intense burning desire to achieve the mission set for you.

The intention of being loved while getting love from the best quality of person.

Not perfect in being but perfect in effort.

Strong in faith in love and head strong with their own intentions and motives

A little bit afraid but confident that the motives are mutual.

Calming and soft yet firm enough to keep everything stable.

A rock you can lean on and a love in which you can draw inspiration.

While giving inspiration as well

Someone with the same soul and heart as yours

The fire that lights you up with excitement

The lighting that strikes and brings you back to life.

The color that splashes on to your once blank canvas

Most simply put.

Your soulmate

What If

What if I showered her with love and gifts.

We talked like forever was it.

Just her and I our four eyes towards the sky

As we confirmed that we waited our whole lives for this

To feel energy from just a kiss

From just a hug just a smile

For no reason just because

Simple as can be but as complex as love.

That we fall into just as deep

Truth be told I'll be glad if you're fearless.

Just something about standing beside you makes me fear less.

I'm a troubled mind but this causes me to feel a high like none other.

It's just something about two people that can stand each other.

That brings peace in my eyes.

Smiles as genuine as a golden brick.

Diamond in the rough it'd be hard to cope if you said no but I had hope.

That this was something more than a back and forth

With more understanding than ever before

If not for real let me know now in case I don't make it tomorrow

Cause I'd rather pass you by and say at least I tried.

Then to lose what I thought I had and think

What If

Trust Me

Tears in my eye's hands held through troubling times.

You look at me while I look you in your eyes and tell you.

Trust Me

Even if it gets harder.

Even if it feels like you can't go any farther

Just climb on my shoulders or jump in my arms.

And I'll make sure we get to where we are going.

Trust me.

Even if I take a beating.

no matter how difficult life may seem.

it's always a way and I won't stop till I find it.

Just trust me.

Let go of your doubts and disbelief.

no matter what doesn't seem clear to me.

I'll make it clear no matter what I'll be here telling you to

Trust Me

To You from Me

To you from me hopefully to brighten your day

Our pain is idle, and we stand together to brighten our way.

To a darkened path I saved a half of love for you to dwell on

Please keep it close and don't leave us alone.

To each is own I didn't settle.

What's mine is yours what's yours is mine no better life.

I place my knee firm in the ground to let you know this love is settled.

With love as strong as gold nimble as water high hopes for future is ours.

Though battered and bruised we'll lace up our boots.

I know this war will bring scars but

As long as promises stay kept, let's take a step for two.

One hop wouldn't be enough.

And a slide just wouldn't make do.

So, to you from me hopefully to brighten your day.

You're my superhero with power of love that stays above the rest.

To you from me of course the course we take is ours to own.

I held you close till you act tough now it's more so a gentle approach.

This is to you from me just to remind you we've found our way.

And if we ever get lost, we'll make a day for love to brighten our day.

Ps. I love you,

-Markeith

Bracing for Love

I'm in love with you.

So, in result I dropped my guard

with no regard

for my broken heart.

I did away with most of my past just as soon as

I started to say hey to you.

Just don't change in exchange for my heart

I'll share my world with you.

Diamonds in roughs all love no bluffs

I won't pretend to act tough when I talk to you.

Giving you this wasn't easy at all

but it feels good bracing for a fall that ends in love.

Thank You for Your Motivation

Dear lady dear woman beautiful woman my special something you're finally here. On good and bad nights, I prayed for you. Although I'm still setting the stage for you. So many false alarms but you're finally here. Bright not just in skin tone but from your mind down to your pure soul. Its genuinely a pleasure to be in your presence and accept the gift of knowing who you are as my special present.

I'm truly grateful, so much that I'll put my all in it to making sure that we fall in it as equals. To give you as much of me as you can handle as we bear witness to a new candle lit with love. From flames we make when we're together. But again, thank you for your motivation. I've longed for it. True appreciation and a reason to go strong for it. For someone. For you. Even if I don't know what we'll become I thank you even if it's just for nothing I thank you. Pretty lady beautiful woman I'm glad you're real. I almost gave up hope on good things. You ignited a flame that's long been extinguished and I'm glad I can feel. So, thank you for being you. It means a lot and I'm glad you took the time to think and said yes to being mine.

Ps. Thank you for your motivation

CPSIA information can be obtained
at www.ICGtesting.com
Printed in the USA
BVRC100921030521
606330BV00004B/151

9781951300746